V I E W F I N D E R

Cut along the appropriate dotted line for
one of the two sizes of viewfinder.

A BRUSH WITH ASHLEY

A BRUSH WITH ASHLEY

—

A Watercolourist's Workbook

Ashley Jackson

Boxtree
in association with

Yorkshire Television Ltd

I dedicate this book to my wife, Anne, and two daughters, Heather and
Claudia, for the love and support that they have given to me along the hills
and valleys of life's highways. This book is also dedicated to Yorkshire,
for inspiring me to paint her.

Front cover: 'Broken Light – Hornby Castle from Tatham'
by Ashley Jackson. Back cover: photograph of Ashley
Jackson courtesy of British Gas

First published in Great Britain in 1993 by Boxtree Limited

Text, Illustrations and Photographs © Ashley Jackson 1993

The right of Ashley Jackson to be identified as Author of this
Work has been asserted by him in accordance with the
Copyright, Designs and Patents Act 1988.

1 2 3 4 5 6 7 8 9 10

Edited by Chris Wood
Designed by Maggie Aldred
Typeset by SX Composing Ltd, Rayleigh, Essex
Colour Origination by Rainbow Graphics, Hong Kong
Printed and bound in Great Britain by Butler and Tanner Ltd,
Frome for   Boxtree Limited
              Broadwall House
              21 Broadwall
              London SE1 9PL

A CIP catalogue entry for this book is available from the British
Library.

ISBN 1 85283 418 8

Contents

Earth, Wind and Fire

INTRODUCTION

A Brush with Ashley is aimed at taking art to the people. All my life I have been involved in art, but have felt that it is enjoyed only by a small minority. With this book, I would like to take art to the majority. Painting open landscape is a two-fold joy, both in trying to capture what you see, and in being able to appreciate Mother Nature herself.

I have been in love with Mother Nature's landscapes since childhood, and it has been my great joy to be able to paint and to teach others – not just how to see the landscape but to observe and represent it.

I am just a simple artist, and I feel that the best way to teach any subject, including painting, is to simplify it. This book has not been written to intimidate, but to encourage you to take up your brush and paint in the great cathedral of the open air. As the Chinese proverb says: 'It is the economy of line that matters.'

This book is targetted at all ages, and at all stages of the learning process. It can be used as a reference book, or as a book on technique that can be taken out into the field. It is designed so that, unlike other books which can only be used indoors, it can be your companion in the world of landscape painting. *A Brush with Ashley* is a book that has been written and designed by a painter for people who paint.

Art materials

The Paper
The foundation of any watercolour painting is the paper. Three kinds of watercolour paper are available:

H.P. (HOT PRESS)
The surface of this paper is very smooth. It is ideal for detailed line and wash work, but I would not recommend it for watercolour painting on location, where you will be using a wet-on-wet technique.

NOT
This paper has a medium surface, the word 'not' meaning not hot press. To avoid confusion, the Americans call this paper 'cold press'. The surface of the paper is textured and gives a beautiful effect when used with paintings or drawings that do not demand great precision.

ROUGH
At 140lbs (300gms) in weight, rough gives you great scope, its texture allowing you to be less precise than you need to be with the other papers. It can create pebbles on a beach, or reflections in water far better.

Notes:
Rag and cotton paper is very expensive, but for location painting I recommend it, and nothing less than 140lbs (300gms) in weight will do. Other papers tend to fur up when using the wet-on-wet technique and the finished product will look overworked.

The three textures of paper are not made to a universal standard, so that one manufacturer's 'rough' can be another's 'not', so you need to know the texture that will suit your work best.

You must practise on the same quality and texture paper that you are going to use for your final painting. If you do not, it is like practising on a cart horse, then jumping on a highly-strung thoroughbred to show. With both you will immediately fall off.

The correct side of the paper is the one with a watermark on it. However, I always use both sides of the paper, on the principle that if it turns out right, it is a painting; if not, it has been practice.

Brushes – The Essential Tools
The brushes that I use and recommend for wet-on-wet landscape painting are as follows:

1.21 A Washbrush – a large 1in (25mm) squirrel hair brush (as in photograph)

1.22 A series number 12 sable
1.23 A series number 10 sable
1.24 A series number 4 sable
1.25 A ¾in (19mm) chisel edge brush

NOTES:

Natural haired brushes should be used at all times. This is the equivalent of preferring a natural sponge over a synthetic one – the real thing holds more water. The diagrams show clearly why natural haired brushes form a reservoir of water much more readily than synthetic. Under a microscope three synthetic hairs will look like **Diagram A**; imagine this to be the hair of your brush, holding globules of water. In **Diagram B**, the three natural hairs, with their split ends, hold water globules in the reservoir of the brush, and more importantly, in the point of the brush. A natural haired brush also releases a lot more water.

The size of my paintings is generally 20 x 30ins (51 x 76cm). As this is quite large, the brushes I recommend are those for large watercolours. If painting on a smaller scale, I advise you to buy brushes two series apart, e.g. a 3, 5 and 7. It is unnecessary to buy every brush available, as a number 6, for example, does more or less what a number 7 can do.

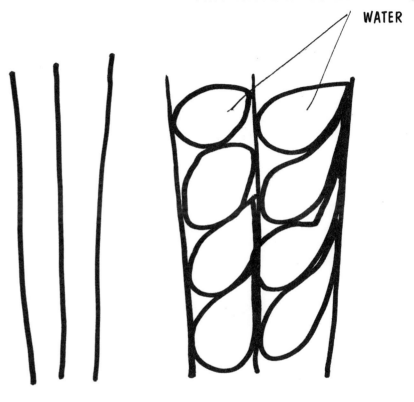

WATER

DIAGRAM A

9

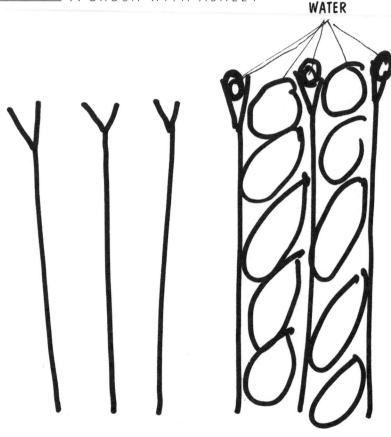

WATER

DIAGRAM B

Paints

There are two standards of watercolour paints, both are available in pan and tube format:

STUDENT – these all cost the same and are made from synthetic materials, so many of the colours are opaque.
ARTIST – these are made from pure pigments, and so vary in price and are more expensive.

NOTES:

I use artist quality tubed paints all the time as they are more transparent, and the glycerine in them enables the paint to flow more easily on the paper. With tubed paint, I find it easier to squirt out the exact amount of colour that I require. With pans of colour, you tend to dirty the colours as you mix them together; the result is painting with coloured water instead of watercolour.

The Palette

It is better to use a metal palette (*see photograph*) rather than a plastic one, for two reasons: first, a plastic palette stains, and second you will have trouble mixing a colour, because on a plastic palette, it tends to form mercury-like beads that run away from the brush. You can also feel the drag of a metal palette, and this will

My materials: from left, a series 12 sable, series 10 sable, series 4 sable, chisel edge brush and washbrush, with two halves of a pencil, paints, a rubber and a palette.

11

give you more confidence and make you more relaxed. Watercolour painting is difficult enough as it is without making it harder for yourself!

Pencils

Use a 4B pencil sharpened with a razor blade and cut in half. Cut it in this way so that you are able to hold it in the palm of your hand as a joiner would. This will give you the full freedom of the wrist, and your drawing will become much looser. Sharpening your pencil with a sharpener is not only wasteful, but gives you a point which is good for writing but not drawing. You can shade in with the edge of a pencil sharpened by razor.

Rubber

A putty rubber is the best type of rubber to use as it is flexible and can be shaped into a point to remove minute details. It is also gentle on the paper.

Water

I suggest you use a child's bucket or a similar container which will hold approximately two pints (1 litre) of water. Take plenty of water with you - enough to be able to change frequently so that your washes are transparent and clear.

Easel

Use a good stout metal easel with a drawing-board. Metal easels will not walk away from you when you are painting. Make your drawing-board out of hardboard rather than wood, as this is lighter to carry on location.

Tape

Use masking tape to tape down your paper.

NOTES:

Good practical warm clothes are essential to making your day out enjoyable. Be prepared for all weathers.

Working Pages

I promised you that this book would be an artist's companion. You will find that opposite and throughout, I have left blank pages. These pages are not printing errors, they are there to provide you with the opportunity and freedom to expand on the techniques I describe and explain in the book. With these personal working pages you will be able to create your own travelling studio and ensure that *A Brush With Ashley* becomes undoubtedly, a true artist's companion.

PERSPECTIVE – Using Your Eyes

We can all relate to the childlike drawing of a house and garden in **Work-out 1**; it is how everyone starts to draw. If you can draw like this you are ready to be introduced to the joys of creating a painting with life, as all that this picture lacks is perspective. Now I can begin to take you on the journey . . .

What is Perspective?

In life we see things as three-dimensional. In art we use perspective to give a subject shape and size, and the *impression* that it is three-dimensional.

Constructing Perspective

In order to construct perspective you need to be able to understand the terms *eye level*, and *vanishing point*, as these are the main tools required.

Many books refer to the eye-level line as the horizon line. This is slightly confusing. The horizon is the line where the landscape meets the sky, and the only time that the eye-level line and the horizon meet is in flat landscape or when looking out to sea. You will be able to see this clearly in **Work-out 2**. Otherwise, your eye-level line and the horizon line are two separate lines altogether as in **Work-out 3**, where the eye-level line is above the subject.

The easiest way to find your eye-level line is to look straight ahead of you. (Make sure it is straight ahead and neither up nor down or your picture will always be twisted.) Where your eyes come to rest is your eye level. I always think of my eye level as a slipped halo across my eyes, and whenever I stand up or sit down my eye level moves with me.

A painting with perspective should also have at least one vanishing point. A vanishing point is where the subject vanishes. For example, imagine two parallel lines going into the distance. They will seem to meet at your eye-level line; this point is the vanishing point.

I hope that the following work-outs will emphasize further the importance of the eye-level line and vanishing point. Look at **Work-out 4**. The tops of the mountains and trees in the distance form the horizon line, and where the road ends is the eye-level line. As

WORKOUT I

WORKOUT 2

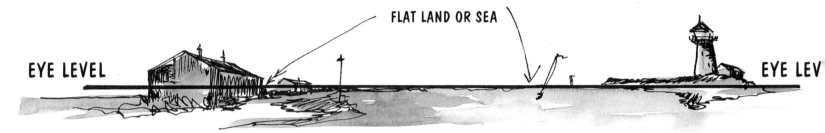

FLAT LAND OR SEA

EYE LEVEL

EYE LEV

EYE LEVEL

WORKOUT 3

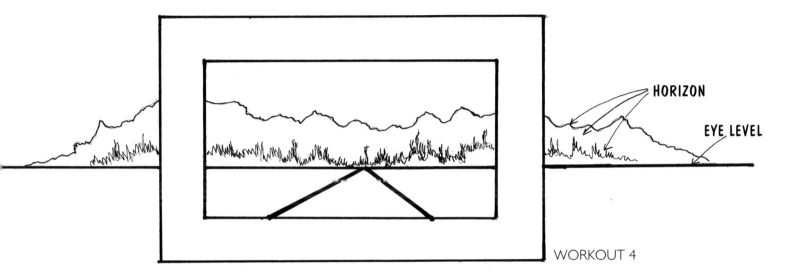

HORIZON

EYE LEVEL

WORKOUT 4

you can see from the diagram your eye-level line continues right outside the picture. The vanishing point in this picture is where the two parallel lines of the road have receded into the distance and formed a point, thus making the road seem to disappear.

Work-out 5 is an example of why a picture should contain more than one vanishing point. When you look closely at this picture you get the feeling that there is an imaginary plug in the centre, and if you were to pull it

out, the painting would drain away and disappear. Try not to make the same mistake; begin the lines within your picture.

Work-out 6 is the correct way to construct perspective. You can see in this work-out that the eye level continues well outside your picture, and your vanishing points end both inside and outside the drawing, so allowing the work-out to become interesting to the eye.

17

VANISHING POINT

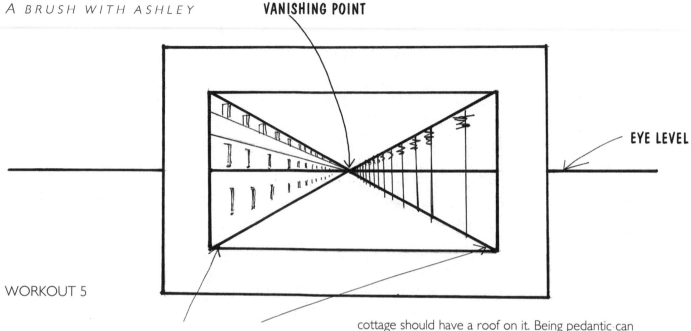

EYE LEVEL

WORKOUT 5

CORNER TO CORNER

When incorporating perspective into a drawing, do not become too technically involved by drawing what you think you can see. For example, consider the cottage in **Work-out 7**. I have tried to draw the gable end and the front of the cottage without a roof, as in **Work-out 6**, but the end result looks as though the

cottage should have a roof on it. Being pedantic can sometimes throw you out because it is easy to forget that perspective straightens itself out at certain distances. Looking at **Work-out 5**, you can see that by straightening out the line, the roof and the gable end come together, giving me the picture that I wanted.

NOTES:
When constructing perspective remember that all vertical lines must stay vertical, any horizontal line above

18

Upper Knowles Farm, high in the Peninnes
The perspective lines of the buildings in this painting hit the eye-level line in several places; each of them draws the eye, giving the composition many vanishing points.

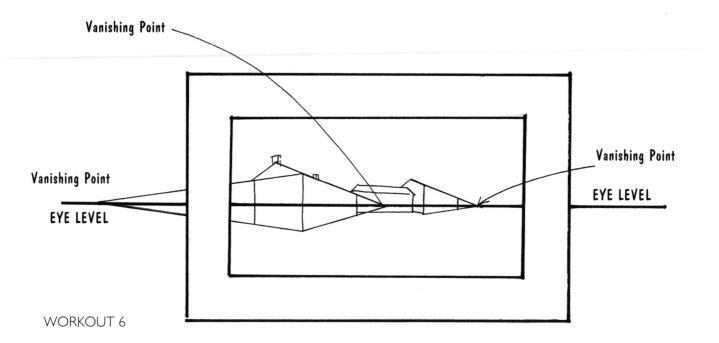

Vanishing Point

Vanishing Point

EYE LEVEL

Vanishing Point

EYE LEVEL

WORKOUT 6

the eye-level line must seem to be drawn down to the eye-level line and any horizontal line below must be drawn up to the eye-level line.

This is one good reason why you should not use a camera to take reference pictures in flat landscape. The camera has no brain. When you aim a camera at the point where your eye-level line and horizontal line meet, the camera will tell the truth as far as perspective goes. But, should you tilt your camera away from the

eye-level line, the vertical line will be distorted. It is for this reason that it is much better to do all your perspective drawings on location rather than back in the studio. Perspective is one of the foundations of a good painting and it is vital that it is correct.

A tip to remember when trying to create distant perspective, say of a tower or church clock, is that distance straightens perspective out the nearer it gets to the eye-level line, up or down, as in **Work-out 8**.

20

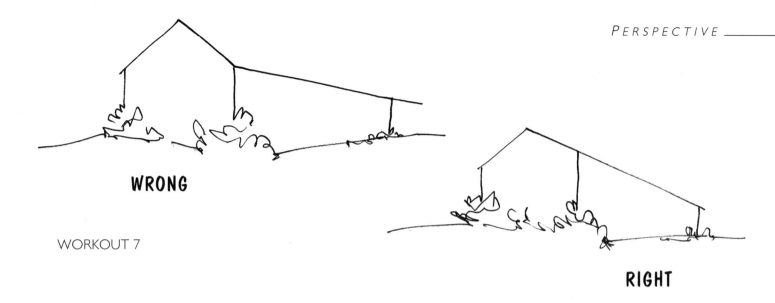

WRONG

WORKOUT 7

RIGHT

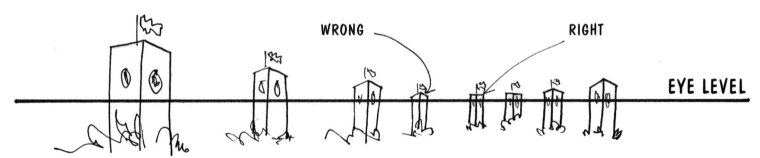

WRONG

RIGHT

EYE LEVEL

WORKOUT 8   21

Composition

If I were to say to a novice, 'paint me that tree you can see in the field', and if they had no idea about composition, they would probably place the tree in the centre of the paper (*see* **Work-out 9**). If you look closely at the picture, however, I think you will find that this makes a very flat painting. Your eyes are attracted immediately to the tree, then bounced straight out again. The reason for this is the unimaginative composition. You have to remember when composing a landscape that you are telling a story. Just as a book seeks to engross the reader, a painting should encourage the viewer to enter its world. In this chapter I discuss why this happens and how to make a picture more interesting.

What is composition?

Throughout this chapter, I prefer to use the word 'composition', from the verb 'to compose', rather than

24 WORKOUT 9

the more clinical 'layout'. We as artists compose paintings, whether topographical or abstract, as a composer composes music. A good composition will guide the viewer's eye into the painting, directing the eye from one part of the painting to another, thereby telling a story and conveying a mood and feeling.

An example of composition would be if you were viewing a landscape, and a tree that you wished to put in the painting lay just outside your frame. You put it in, thereby composing the landscape.

The Ashley Jackson Approach to simple composition

There are various mathematical ways of composing your painting. Having worked as an apprentice in a studio where we did lettering of all types with a brush, I have devised a simple method, using the letters L, U, X and Z, for use in the composition of your landscape paintings.

L COMPOSITION

Work-out 10 shows a cottage, trees and landscape, which I have composed using the letter L. The cottage and the trees are the leg of the L, and the path and field going into the distance form the foot of the L. This gives

a nice balance and the eye is kept interested in the painting. As you can see from **Work-out 11**, the L can work just as well when reversed.

Work-out 12 is another simple L-shaped composition. With the fells beyond, the clouds in the sky guide your eye down into the painting.

U COMPOSITION

This is a difficult composition, for if done incorrectly, as in **Work-out 13**, it splits the painting in two, with a subject on either side and nothing in the middle. It is as bad to have nothing in the centre as it is to have something. The French impressionists knew how to break the rules in a U-shaped composition, by reserving one side of the painting for cold colours, and the other for warm, hence forming a double L composition (*see* **Work-out 14**). I will discuss this further in Chapter 4, which is about tonal value.

Z COMPOSITION

The Z composition can be done in reverse too, the format drawing your eye into the picture very easily. In **Work-out 15** it is the clouds which draw us in. In **Work-out 16** your eyes will run along the foreground, hit the post in the corner, and then be directed towards

WORKOUT 11

27

WORKOUT 12

WORKOUT 14

WORKOUT 15

WORKOUT 16

WORKOUT 17

the lighthouse. You then travel into the clouds, and a Z-shaped composition is formed, sandwiching the picture and keeping your eyes within it.

X COMPOSITION

Work-out 17 shows an X-shaped composition. The subject is in the centre so that, when you look at the painting, your gaze is immediately bounced out again.

DOUBLE L COMPOSITION

Work-out 18 shows a double L composition. The trees and foreground form one L, and the building and landscape behind form a second. This allows you to look at the tree on the right-hand side first, taking in the cottage at the same time, and then following the direction of the arrows into the distance. This keeps your eyes trained on the painting. Your point of escape, which we discuss further in Chapter 10, is at its centre.

NOTES:

In getting your composition correct, always remember that when painting landscape you can have one-third landscape and two-thirds sky, or vice versa (see **Work-outs 19** and **20**). When you are starting out, it is a good idea to have one-third land and two-thirds sky for flat landscape, and one-third sky and two-thirds land for hilly landscape. However, when you have mastered this

33

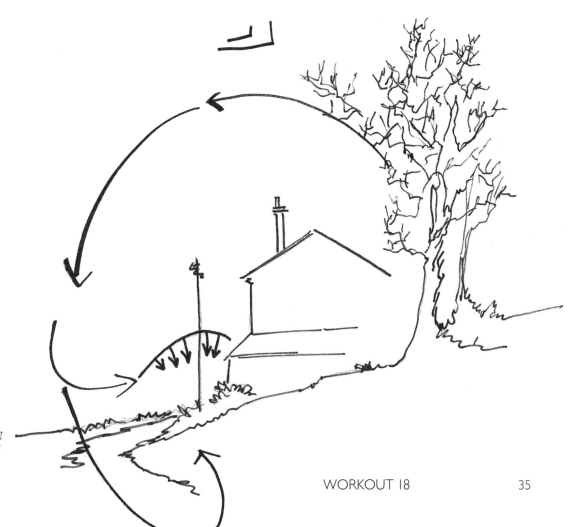

◄ Roxby Beck, Staithes

This is an L-shaped composition with the L in reverse. The buildings on the right form the leg of the L while the heavy shadows and reflection on the rocks and water form the foot. All this frames the distant view.

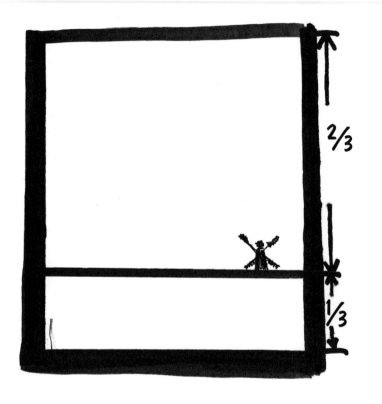

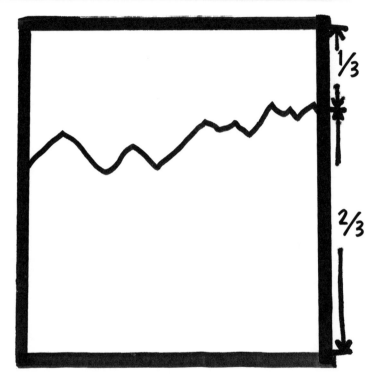

WORKOUT 19

WORKOUT 20

technique, you could try two-thirds land in flat landscape. What you must not do (*see* **Work-out 21**) is to divide your paper into equal sections. This effectively splits the picture in half and produces a boring result. You may be confused when asked whether you paint on landscape or portrait paper. The difference is simple: when the paper is horizontal, it is 'landscape' (**Work-out 22**); when vertical, it is 'portrait' (**Work-out 23**). A good composition tip when painting from a car is clearly illustrated here. In **Work-out 24**, the car is parked on the nearside of the road and the artist (in the driving seat) is too near the centre of the road. The result is likely to be a poor X composition, In **Work-out 25**, the driver is nearer the verge, away from the centre of the composition, and is less likely to produce a corner-to-corner composition. Note the two photographs of a winter scene. **Photograph A** is wrong. It is weak because the tree is the focal point in the centre of the picture. In **Photograph B**, the tree is to the left, thereby opening up the view, with the wall taking you right into the distance. On close examination, I would call this an L-shaped composition.

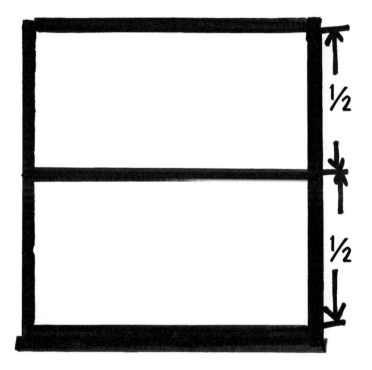

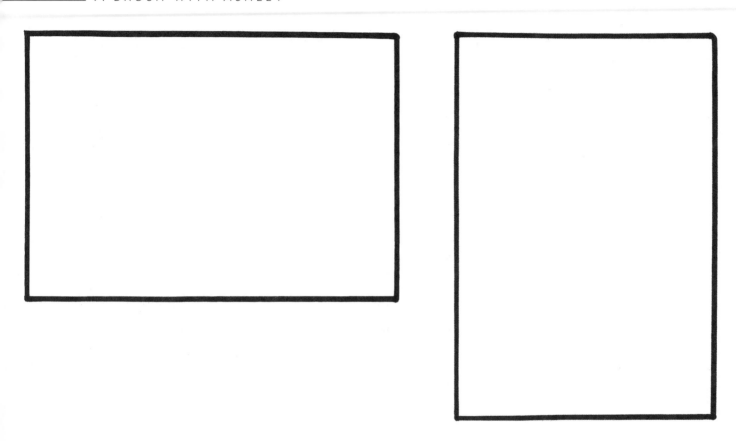

WORKOUT 22   WORKOUT 23

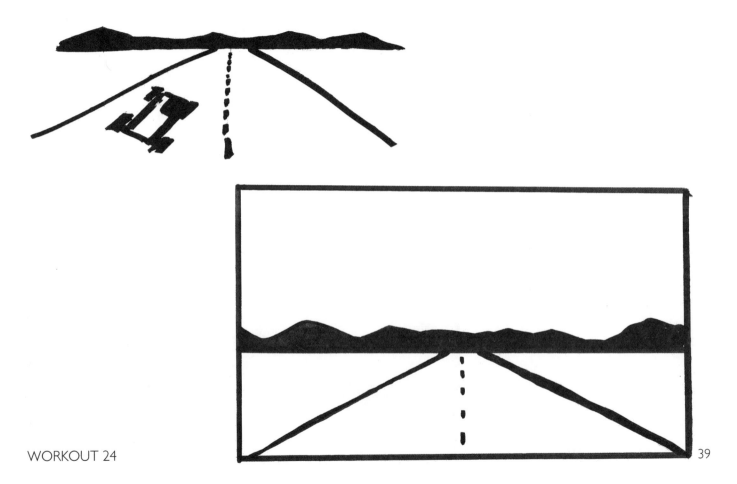

WORKOUT 24

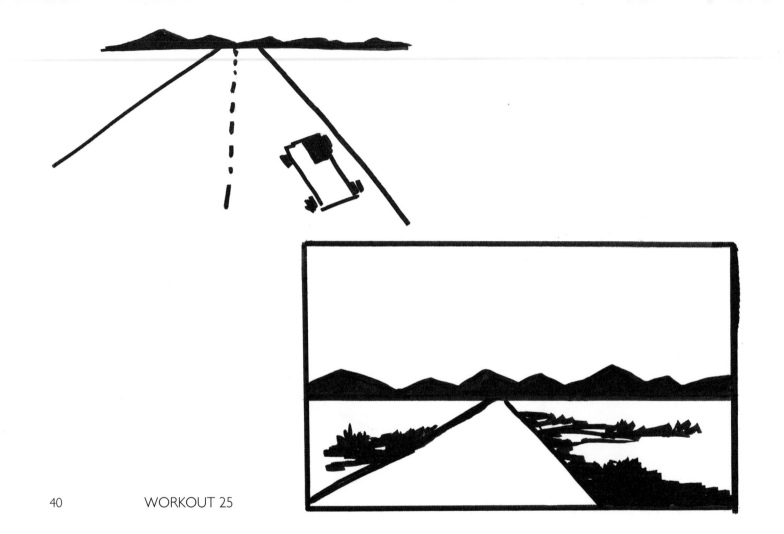

WORKOUT 25

PHOTOGRAPH   A

PHOTOGRAPH   B

TONAL VALUE – Monochromes

Ask a painter who is ignorant about tonal value to paint a house or an apple, and the result will be flat and shapeless, a mere outline, or what I call an 'outline-tinted drawing'. **Work-out 26** lacks all tonal value; **Work-out 27**, however, uses tonal value to give shape and depth to the picture. The effect is achieved by the presence of a source of light which is not present in **Work-out 26**. It is by knowing the origin of the light in your picture that you will achieve shape.

What is tonal value?

Tonal value is the light and shade that gives a two-dimensional shape to your painting. To understand the concept better, stand outside and look into the distance. You will notice that the contrast between light and shade is less marked the further you look, the lights becoming weaker and the shades softer. Anything in the foreground, on the other hand, displays greater contrast, the lights and darks both exaggerated. The snow in the photograph **Snow in Wharfedale** has helped make this a monochromatic picture, getting rid of colour, and just showing tone. This photograph demonstrates tonal value.

To understand tones further, look at **Valley of the tones** (see page 49). On the left of the page you will see my depiction of a valley with foreground, middle distance and distance, the tones taken from the band of tones on the right-hand side. The sharp dark tones of the foreground have been taken from the bottom of the band of tones, and the rest follow in sequence. The top of the band of tones is therefore the horizon in the landscape.

I suggest that you use this tone chart when you are out painting. Hold the page up in front of you, lining up the edge of the paper with the subject, and close your left eye. Then match the tone on the chart to the tone you are trying to paint. This visual aid will help you to understand the meaning of tonal value.

The only way to learn how to achieve shape and depth is through creating *monochromes* – paintings or drawings achieved by using just one colour. Both **Work-out 26** and **Work-out 27** are monochromes.

WORKOUT 26

45

WORKOUT 27

Snow in Wharfedale

Look carefully at **Work-out 29** and you will see that, although it depicts nothing except pure monochrome washes, I have been able to create a feeling of depth. The tones weaken in order to imply distance, and the feeling of depth is achieved by contrasting weak and strong tones.

I cannot emphasize enough the importance of practising monochromes. Monochromes are to an artist what scales are to a musician: they may seem tedious, but master them and you will be well on the way to creating a painting that is interesting and eyecatching.

In my experience, the student who has not grasped tonal value wil never be able to achieve a pure watercolour. The tell-tale giveaway is the student who has to outline everything: do this and you will create an outlined tinted drawing – not a watercolour.

NOTES:

Always include a light source in your paintings. When painting outside, the source of light changes constantly. To 'chase' the light, however, is to court disaster. Instead, freeze the light source before you start painting, marking the direction of the light with arrows on the border of your picture (*see* **Work-out 30**). These will help you to achieve the necessary shape and depth.

Something to remember when trying to understand monochromes is that a black and white movie is a monochrome. When watching old movies, study the tones and you will soon start to appreciate the varying depths of a monochrome.

I practise monochromes every week without fail. There is no easier way of getting to grips with tonal value.

DO NOT MOVE ON TO THE NEXT CHAPTER UNTIL YOU HAVE THOROUGHLY MASTERED THE MONOCHROME.

WORKOUT 29

LIGHT?

COLOUR PERSPECTIVE and STABLES of COLOUR

In Chapter 3 you may recall that I referred to the French impressionists and how they made a U-shaped composition seem correct. One side of the avenue of trees say, or the U, would be painted in a warm colour, and the other in a cool or cold colour, hence giving the feeling of a double L composition (see Chapter 3, **Work-out 18**). By using cold and warm tones the impressionists made their paintings interesting. It is because of their knowledge of colour perspective that they could attempt this type of composition.

Colour perspective is vitally important and I hope that the following exercises will make it easier to understand. When you have completed them you should no longer be frightened about the use of colour in your painting. Please note that many books refer to colour perspective as aerial perspective. I find this terminology confusing – it seems to imply that you need an airplane!

Colour perspective

Work-out 31 shows a pair of rectangles, one blue and the other red. Train your eye on them. The red rectangle appears to be placed up against the blue one, giving the impression that there is no space between the two blocks, which appear completely flat. The same effect occurs in **Work-out 32**. The mountains in the background dominate the painting and make the background and foreground appear to be on the same plane. In other words, the painting looks flat and uninteresting; the colour perspective in both cases is wrong.

But why? I hear you ask yourself. The reason is that red is a warm colour and so advances; and blue is a cold colour and so retreats. In both **Work-outs 31** and **32**, the red is trying to push itself forward, climbing over the blue. Putting red in the background of your painting and blue in the foreground will always make the background jump forward to merge with the foreground and because of this the painting will become flat and distorted.

Now look at **Work-out 33**, where the red block is in the foreground, and the blue is in the background. With this work-out you should get a feeling of the space behind the two rectangles. You should sense that the blue block continues behind the red. This work-out shows the correct method for achieving colour perspective. Using the warmth of the colour red in the foreground and the cool of blue in the distance, the picture gives true colour perspective, as does **Work-out 34**. With blue mountains in the background and the red in the foreground, the painting gains depth. In this example, the mountains retreat and the foreground advances, and the painting appears to be on two planes. As you can see, using colour perspective correctly makes the painting more attractive to the eye; you are led in by the foreground, and your eye is held by the painting.

NOTES:

Red is warm colour and so advances; blue is a cold colour and so retreats. Therefore, reds should be used for foreground and middle distance; blues for distance.

Warm and cold tones

In the last chapter, when I talked about tonal value, I did not discuss warm tones and cold tones, as I believe an understanding of colour perspective is necessary first. Now, however, I can introduce two more valleys for you to use as practical aids when out painting on location. The **Valley of warm tones** (see page 55) and the **Valley of cold tones** (see page 59) are to be used like the **Valley of tones** in the previous chapter, but you are now at the stage to take your tones a step further. Use the **Valley of warm tones** on page 55 as your guide to foreground and middle distance, and the **Valley of cold tones** on page 59 for background and distance.

A good tip, which has worked well for me when I have been looking into the far distance of the landscape, and then trying to capture it on paper, is to try and imagine that every fifty feet (8 metres) away there is a coloured sheet of blue or grey glass. The further you look into the distance, the more sheets of glass you will be looking at. This is clearly illustrated by the photograph of **Buckstones**. This will help you achieve colour perspective. And, once you have mastered colour perspective, you should be ready to grasp the magnificent art of colour.

Buckstones

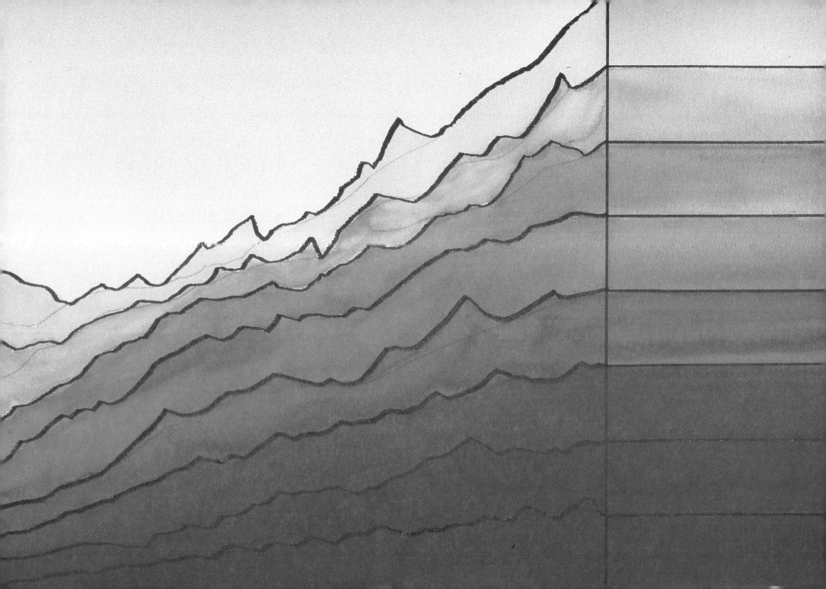

WORKOUT 31

58   WORKOUT 32

Stables of Colour

When walking into an art shop and looking at the colour range, you are likely to be as bamboozled and shellshocked by the great range available to you as I am. When you enquire what difference there is between the colours Prussian Blue and Ultramarine Blue, for example, you will get the answer, 'I like them both'; and you will be left none the wiser!

The first thing to remember is that there are only three primary colours: blue, yellow and red. The true group of primary colours, in which you can see no other colour, comprises cobalt blue, cadmium red and cadmium yellow. All other colours are secondary colours and are obtained from mixing the primary colours, for example red and blue to make purple, blue and yellow to give green, and yellow and red for orange.

So that you can relax and enjoy more fully the art of watercolour, I have devised what I call my **Stable of colours**. This should enable you to get to grips with the art of colour mixing. You should be able to create a painting by using just three colours – red, yellow and blue – so I have created three stables of colours, as seen in **Work-out 38**, **Stables A, B** and **C**. In each of these three stables there is a different red, yellow and blue. Study the stables, and then, using the same composition, paint three different studies, one with each stable. To make things easier, I have suggested a composition in **Work-out 39**.

STABLE A WORK-OUT

This stable comprises the three primary colours: cobalt blue, cadmium yellow and cadmium red.

STABLE B WORK-OUT

Here I have used Prussian Blue, Lemon Yellow and Burnt Sienna. You will note that Prussian Blue is a cold blue, as it has some yellow in it, giving it a green tinge. Lemon Yellow has a tint of blue in it, making it a cold yellow, and Burnt Sienna contains a hint of yellow, making it a cool red. This work-out gives a fresh, cool impression.

STABLE C WORK-OUT

The three colours in this work-out are Ultramarine Blue, Raw Sienna and Crimson Alizarin. The work-out has a much warmer feel than the **Stable B work-out** because it is made up of warmer colours: Ultramarine Blue has some red in it, as does Raw Sienna. Crimson Alizarin, on the other hand, contains blue, making it a cold red.

NOTES:

The stables that I have given are merely guidelines, but by using these, with practice you will master the art of colour mixing. Use these stables as your guide, and when you feel ready, use the blank **Work-out 40** to draw your own composition and mix the stables together. Once you have learnt the rules you will have much more fun breaking them!

Rather than buy a full set of student-quality paints I recommend that you buy nine artist-quality tubes of paint with which to learn your colour mixing.

Key Colours

I have heard students out on location say, while looking at a wooded valley, for example: 'There are so many greens in the scene.' They are then frightened to death by the prospect of colour-mixing the scene. I prefer to say that there are many yellows in the vista, but there is only one blue.

It is vital for your painting to have a key colour. If you study any great painting you will get the impression that the painting has been completed at one moment in time on one day, not that the sky was painted in the morning, the background in the afternoon and the foreground and middle distance in the evening, as was generally the case. This is because the great painters have always incorporated a key colour in their paintings.

Your source of light is the sky, and whatever colour the sky is on the day you are going to paint, you should drop a little of that colour into all the other colours you are mixing for your landscape. This will be your key colour. You need only a pin-head of the key colour in your mixes; use it sparingly as a chef would use salt in his cooking. If you do this, your painting will have harmony, the feeling that it was created on one day at one moment in time. The viewer will not have the impression that the sky is in Madrid, the distance in Cornwall and the foreground in Yorkshire!

Here are six work-outs to demonstrate this theory to you. In **Work-outs 41, 42** and **43**, I have used the same yellows throughout – Lemon Yellow, Cadmium Yellow and Raw Sienna – but in each of the exercises I have changed the key colour blue. You can easily see the difference in tone and atmosphere the key colour makes. In **Work-out 41**, the key colour Prussian Blue has been used by itself, as a monochrome. Prussian Blue, a cold blue, gives a nice snowy winter's scene. Ultramarine Blue is the key colour used in **Work-out 42**. This gives a warmer feel to a winter's scene than does Prussian Blue. Cobalt Blue, the key colour of

WORKOUT 33

WORKOUT 34

WORKOUT 38A

COBALT BLUE

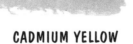

CADMIUM YELLOW

CADMIUM RED

63

WORKOUT 38B

WORKOUT 38C

ULTRAMARINE BLUE

RAW SIENNA

CRIMSON ALIZARIN

67

WORKOUT 39

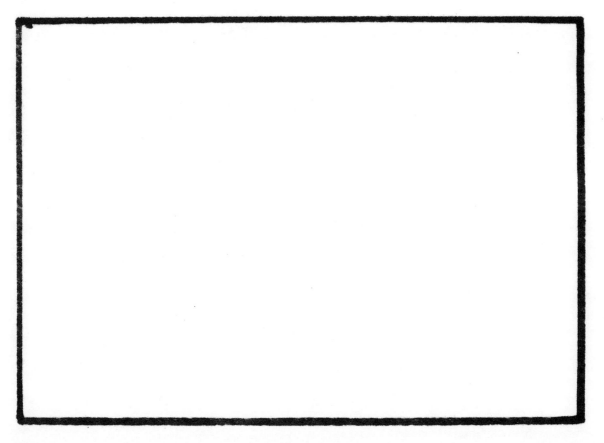

WORKOUT 40

PRUSSIAN BLUE   LEMON YELLOW   CADMIUM YELLOW   RAW SIENNA

Work-out 43, is an intermediate between the two blues used previously.

This is a simple exercise. Once mastered, you can start to introduce several blues in one painting. However, make sure one of those blues is your key colour.

NOTES:

In these exercises I have used the three yellows – Lemon Yellow, Cadmium Yellow and Raw Sienna. I prefer using Raw Sienna to Yellow Ochre as Raw Sienna has a little red in it, making it a warm yellow. When painting sky, adding Yellow Ochre to blue washes gives the impression of green. This does not happen with Raw Sienna. The small amount of red contained in it prevents the sky turning green until much more has been added.

Before moving on to the chapter on techniques, make sure you have practised and understood all the previous chapters. If not, you will be painting outline-tinted drawings and calling these line and wash when they are no more than cartoons. Some people would have you believe you can be Rembrandt in a day; this is not true. It is vital that you do not attempt to run before you can walk confidently.

70

FRENCH ULTRAMARINE **LEMON YELLOW** **CADMIUM YELLOW** **RAW SIENNA**

COBALT BLUE **LEMON YELLOW** **CADMIUM YELLOW** **RAW SIENNA**

71

TECHNIQUES

The way you handle art tools is very important. Your brushes are as important to you as a scalpel is to a surgeon. This is why I have always admired the Chinese, who have striven throughout the centuries to master the art of handling a brush. They do it with exceptional brilliance.

I was fortunate enough to spend my childhood years in the Orient. As a child I was fascinated to watch shopkeepers writing with their hog-hair brushes and black ink. They were artists themselves.

The Chinese paint watercolours flat on a table, and their brushes are held vertically at right angles to the paper. By painting in this way, and by carefully judging the amount of pressure they are using, they can swiftly change a thick line to a thin line with one stroke. European watercolourists have always painted at an angle of 45 degrees. The European brush therefore is designed to be able to cope at that angle, wearing to an even shape. The problems come when a novice uses an oriental hog-hair brush for painting watercolours at 45 degrees, used this way, the rhythm and flow is knocked out of the brush.

In all my paintings I use European-style watercolour brushes. As I said in the earlier chapter on materials, it is very important to use natural hair brushes, which are subtle and react instantly to the handler. Synthetic brushes do not. For me, using a synthetic brush is like using a feather to hit a ball.

As you learn to apply varying pressure to your brush, you will come to appreciate just what a European-style watercolour brush can achieve. In the following work-outs you can see clearly what effects are possible with certain brushes.

Brush Effects

In **Work-out 44**, I used a flat ¾in (19mm) brush. By applying it at different angles I can gain many different effects, and from these it is possible to develop telegraph poles, reflections, dry grass, window panes, bricks, and much more.

In **Work-out 45**, a number 10 pointed sable was used. With this brush you can paint waves, telegraph poles and grass. Note the difference between **Work-outs 44** and **45**; this is due to the different shaped brushes.

In **Work-out 46**, I have used my favourite washbrush, a 1in (25mm) squirrel filbet. A filbet brush is

WORKOUT 44

WORKOUT 45

WORKOUT 46

a chisel-edged brush with the corners cut off. Many washbrushes made today can only be used for applying washes, but, as you can see from the work-outs, this brush can give you fences, reflections, tufts and clumps of grass, as well as the all-important wash for skies and large areas of painting.

In **Work-out 47**, you will see that I have put on a wash, then pulled the colour off with the washbrush to form clouds. In **Work-out 48**, I have used the washbrush almost dry. This gives the effect of pebbles on a beach and reflections or ripples on water.

I have used a ¾in (19mm) chisel brush in **Work-out 49**. This brush has not only put on the wash, it has also pulled out the colour, forming highlights. In **Work-out 50**, I have used the ¾in (19mm) chisel dry.

A number 14 pointed sable was used in **Work-outs 51** and **52**. In **Work-out 51**, the brush was used for drawing, and in **Work-out 52** it was used dry.

Try these exercises yourself, getting to grips with exactly what effect each brush can achieve. This will give you confidence when tackling your own paintings.

Notes:

When buying brushes, always choose the next series up from the one you were initially going to purchase. A large brush will do what a small brush can, but a small brush cannot achieve all that a large brush can. For instance, in **Work-out 51** a number 14 brush can be used like a number 10 for drawing, but it can also do washes and dry washes as shown in **Work-out 52**, which a smaller brush would have difficulty achieving.

Handling Your Brush

Handling the brushes correctly is a question of craftsmanship. You become a craftsperson when you know and can correctly handle the tools of your trade. There is nothing I admire more than a craftsperson at work, their tools working as part of their body, moving in harmony with the brain, the eye and the hand.

In **Work-out 53**, I have used the colours Prussian Blue, Cadmium Yellow and Crimson Alizerin. Using a 'curved' technique with the washbrush, I have introduced tufts of grass on the right-hand side of the moorland scene, while using the same washbrush for the rest of the area.

In **Work-out 54**, the colours are French Ultramarine Blue, Crimson Alizerine and Cadmium Yellow, and the chisel-edged brush was used for the entire work-out. You will see, in the left foreground, the dry-brush technique used to create blades of grass, which I have

WORKOUT 47

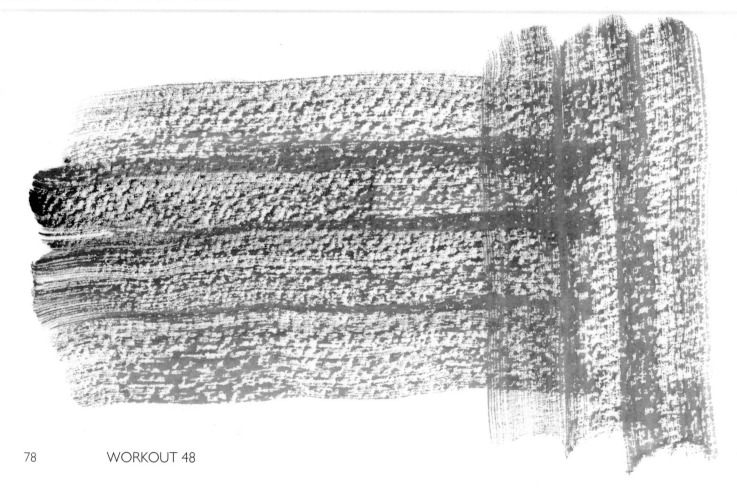

WORKOUT 48

WORKOUT 49

WORKOUT 50

WORKOUT 51

WORKOUT 52

WORKOUT 53

WORKOUT 54

WORKOUT 55

86

WORKOUT 56

then incorporated into the work-out.

Prussian Blue, Cadmium Yellow and Burnt Sienna were used in **Work-out 55**, applied with two entirely different brushes in this exercise, the washbrush and the chisel-edged brush. I used the washbrush both to put the washes in and to paint the clumps of grass. The chisel-edged brush was used for the blades of grass, trees and reflections.

In **Work-out 56**, I have used French Ultramarine Blue, Prussian Blue, Burnt Sienna and Cadmium Yellow. With a chisel-edged brush I pulled out highlights and the same brush was applied for darks and lights. By doing this, I have created a jungle of grass with depths of light and dark tone.

Finally, in this techniques chapter, here are three work-outs using three different technical approaches to watercolour for you to practise. In these exercises I have used only three colours – Ultramarine Blue, Lemon Yellow and Burnt Sienna – and tried to keep my approach as simple as possible.

First I have drawn a country scene, then divided it into three sections. In **Work-out 57**, I have painted the scene as a monochrome. In the other two work-outs, I have taken the Ultramarine Blue into the sky and house. In **Work-out 58**, I mixed the three colours on the actual paper, which gives it a more vibrant feeling than in **Work-out 59**, in which I mixed my colours in the palette to give a much more romantic and softer feel. Try all of these exercises – the monochrome, mixing colour on the actual paper, and then mixing colour in your palette. You will find that there is no reason why you cannot use all of these methods in one painting.

NOTES:

Always remember that, when painting watercolour, you are putting one wash on top of another, like painting with coloured sheets of glass. The old masters who painted in oils used the same technique but called the washes glazes. This method of applying colour gave depth to their paintings.

West Nab
The sharp white highlights in the picture on page 90 were achieved by leaving the paper unpainted; the softer highlights were pulled out of the colour with a moist chisel-edged brush. I used the same brush to paint the jungle of grass in the foreground, giving it depth with dark and light tones.

ULTRAMARINE BLUE   **LEMON YELLOW**   **BURNT SIENNA**

WORKOUT 57, 58, 59

SKIES

Skies Speak to You

Many students and amateurs pay less attention to the sky than to anything else. Their skies are incidental to the painting, often just clear blue or tinted white, which to my mind is boring and lacks atmosphere and movement.

As the sky usually takes up one- to two-thirds of the painting and therefore has an important part to play in the overall effect the painting has on its viewer, this is surprising. The sky is the soul of your landscape – you are after all painting in 'God's cathedral of the open air'. The sky is the spirit and message conveyed by the mood of the landscape; a still sky gives the feeling of serenity, while a stormy sky imposes a sense of wildness on the landscape.

Because the sky is a continually moving landscape, a novice will often find it difficult to paint. And because the novice cannot paint it, he or she does not like to try. If they could, they would really enjoy it.

Skies are vitally important in a landscape. The sky is your source of light; without light your painting would have no tone or colour. And it is from your sky that you derive your key colour.

Work-out 60 clearly shows the tonal value of a sky, with its foreground, middle distance and distance. Remember that the clouds nearest to your head form the foreground of your painting; they will then recede into the distance getting smaller and weaker.

Work-out 61 is an exercise in how to achieve depth in your skies. I have used the colours Prussian Blue, Burnt Sienna and Raw Sienna in the dropcloth of the sky (the wash) and you will see that I have broken the rule of colour perspective. At the top of the painting I have put the foreground of the sky in a cool colour. It is a dark blue giving way to a weaker blue and then merging at the eye level into the warm Raw Sienna background. When the backcloth was dry, I painted my foreground, middle distance and distance clouds on top. You will note that I have used Raw Sienna instead of Yellow Ochre and the sky has not turned green.

In **Work-out 62** you will see a simple sky depicting light rain, which to a landscape painter is known as moorland grit. Burnt Sienna was used to create light rain falling at an angle. To execute this effect put on a wash of clean water, then, dropping the brush in at the top of your painting and using it in windscreen wiper fashion,

WORKOUT 93

WORKOUT 61

WORKOUT 62

obtain the effect of white clouds in your sky, clean your washbrush out immediately and pull out the blue, leaving the white of the paper to show through and thus form clouds.

NOTES:

I paint in the style of the English school of artists, in that I do not use white paint. The use of white paint in a

WORKOUT 63

apply Burnt Sienna, moving the brush down from the strongest to the weakest tone.

After you have done this, pull the brush down at an angle across your paper to achieve the effect of sheets of rain.

I used French Ultramarine Blue in **Work-out 63**. Apply your wash in windscreen wiper fashion so that you have strong colour at the top, getting weaker as you work your way down with the washbrush. To

watercolour immediately makes it opaque and gives the painting body colour, not transparency, giving the impression it has been painted in gouache.

It would pay you to do as Constable and Turner did: practise skyscapes without any land. This will make you observe the different qualities, moods and patterns of the sky. Then show these exercises to a friend and ask what feeling they get out of the skies you have created.

Sky Moods

Here is a collection of skies for you to look at. **Work-out 64** is a moody summer sky; you can feel that it has foreground, middle distance and distance. **Work-out 65** is a windy sky, painted at an angle to give plenty of movement within it. **Work-out 66** is a summer evening sky. To achieve this, I first laid down a background wash, leaving a blank area the size of a small coin for the sun. I then superimposed the warm clouds, again leaving the white coin-sized area. When all was dry, I tinted the sun using the background colour.

Work-out 67 I call my 'cloud burst'. You should feel that if you were to go out walking under a sky like this, your socks would soon become sodden. I achieved this effect by first wetting the whole surface with clean water, then putting the colour in from the top, and

bringing it two-thirds of the way down the sky. I added some warm tones, which were worked with the washbrush to give curtains of rain. In other words, this sky was created by using a wet-on-wet technique.

Once you have grasped and feel totally confident with these sky exercises, you will be ready to marry them with your earth landscapes, as I have done in **Work-outs 68, 69, 70** and **71**.

Work-out 68 shows a light-coloured house with a strong sky, achieved by applying the paint to dry paper.

For **Work-out 69**, wet the surface first, then put the sky in all the way through the landscape. I allowed this to dry before putting in the foreground and distance.

For **Work-out 70**, I wet the paper with clean water and then applied colour all over it. With a clean washbrush, I pulled out the clouds, putting in the foreground of the landscape when all was dry.

For **Work-out 71**, I wet the whole area first with clean water, then dropped in colour from the top, using a windscreen wiper motion to pull it down into the landscape. Again, I put in the landscape when it was dry.

All of these exercises are observations. It is most important to practise observational exercises, especially as far as skies are concerned. As I said earlier, skies are the spiritual essence of your painting.

WORKOUT 64

WORKOUT 65

WORKOUT 66

WORKOUT 67

WORKOUT 68

WORKOUT 69

WORKOUT 70

WORKOUT 71

DETAILS

Oscar Wilde used to say that detail could be vulgar. I am inclined to agree with him; there is nothing better than leaving something to the imagination. Throughout this chapter, I will try and simplify the art of detail – an apparent contradiction in itself!

I find that students love to begin their paintings with a small fine brush, putting in detail before they have even constructed the painting. Having hold of that small fine brush, they dare not let go, and begin to call it 'their favourite brush'. You should always begin a painting with a large brush, putting in the areas of wash, and working down from the large brush to smaller brushes.

You should never do details until you are about to sign your name. First, you must do the part you do not like doing – the large areas.

My grandfather, although not a painter, painted a picture in my mind that I remember every time I eat an apple pie, and it is very apt for this chapter. I used to eat the centre of the pie first, leaving the crust until last, and then, hoping that nobody would see me, I would throw away the crust. On one occasion, he spotted me and asked me why I did it. My answer was simple: 'Because I like the centre and hate the crust.' His homespun reply was: 'Eat the crust first and you will enjoy the centre all the more.' These words have stayed with me ever since. In this case, the detail is the centre of the pie. The detail is to me like the shoelace on a boot, it pulls everything together.

I have divided up this chapter to deal with different areas of detail that will be of interest to you.

Trees

There are three basic shapes of tree that I have tried to simplify for you in **Work-out 72**: an umbrella, a lampshade and a teardrop. The umbrella tree should give you the impression of weeping willows and oak trees; the lampshade, elms and sycamores; and the teardrop, poplars and Christmas trees.

I have painted these trees without leaves. When putting foliage on a tree, you must paint the foliage first, or the trunk will bleed through, giving the impression that the tree has been cut down the centre. When painting foliage, leave gaps for the trunk and branches and then paint these in.

Incidentally, leaving gaps in the foliage not only helps you to see the branches, but stops the birds from

WORKOUT 72

WORKOUT 73

WORKOUT 74

breaking their necks when flying through them!

As the trunk and branches of a tree grow away from you they get thinner and weaker. Do not paint from thin to thick as this does not go with the flow of the tree. The tree grows from the ground, so paint it from the ground up into the sky, as I have done in **Work-out 73**. **Work-out 74** was painted from the top downwards and is incorrect. The reason this will not work is that the human hand shakes until it makes contact with the paper. If you start at the top, with the twigs, your hand will shake and leave blobs, giving the impression that the tree is crowded with budgerigars! Another problem with not starting from the bottom is that you will construct trees, such as those in **Work-out 75**, which look like a rope unwinding.

Working in a commercial art studio was one of my greatest pieces of fortune. It was in this trade that I learnt about the techniques of lettering. I have referred to the use of letters in the previous chapter on composition, and I now refer to it again, this time in connection with the technique of painting trees.

The letters U and V should be rough guides for you when painting trees. To convey to the viewer the strength of a tree you should have U shapes at the bottom of your trunk, as in **Work-out 76**. The U

WORKOUT 75

WORKOUT 76

WORKOUT 77

shape subconsciously makes you feel as though you can climb the tree, unlike the tree in **Work-out 77**, where the V shape of the trunk gives you the feeling that if you were to climb it, it would snap. Vs should be used for painting twigs, as in **Work-out 78**.

Remember that, as with skies in the previous chapter, trees must always have a foreground, middle distance and distance in order to give the impression of depth. **Work-out 79** shows a hand which lacks depth, but **Work-out 80**, a painting of two hands, gives depth through the use of light and shade. **Work-out 81** shows the tree work-out come to life; the foreground branches are dark and sharply defined and the middle distance and distance get progressively weaker.

NOTES:

When you paint trees in a hilly landscape you will notice that if a tree is on the far side of a crag, as in **Work-out 82**, the prevailing winds coming up the crag will clip the tree, preventing it growing above the crag.

Another observation I made while travelling was that children who live in dense jungle will draw something like **Work-out 83** when asked to draw a tree. This is because they can see only the huge roots and trunk of the tree and not the top of it. Children living in open

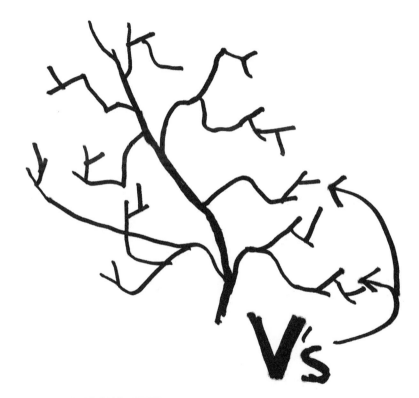

WORKOUT 78

113

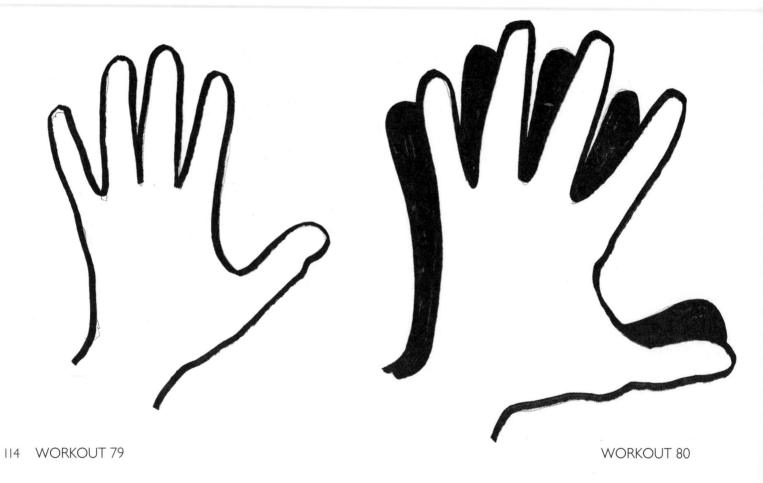

WORKOUT 80

areas paint the whole of the tree.

Work-out 84 shows some observations of trees which use the techniques I have been speaking about, including the shapes U and V. The colours I have used are Prussian Blue, Burnt Sienna, Crimson Alizarin and Lemon Yellow. Note the different trees that can be achieved using our three shapes; here we have an elm, a fir, a silver birch, and a mountain rowan forced to grow in its shape by prevailing winds. Foreground, middle distance and distance are shown clearly in the leaves.

Gates

When painting gates, always remember to leave them slightly open. Do not do as I have in **Work-out 85**, and paint a gate closed. In this exercise, the viewer is led from the path to the gate, but then is brought to a stop, not knowing whether to jump over the gate or smash it down and go through. Nine times out of ten, the viewer's eye, being lazy, will reject the picture as it is led out of it by the walls.

   With the gate left open, as in **Work-out 86**, the viewer's eye is encouraged to travel up to the gate, through it, and further into the picture.

WORKOUT 81

'WIND'

WORKOUT 82

WORKOUT 83

WORKOUT 84

119

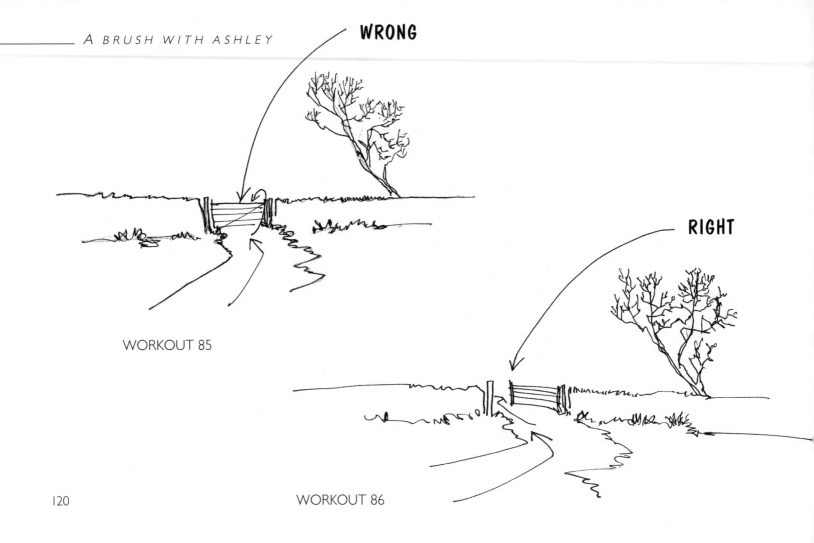

WRONG

RIGHT

WORKOUT 85

WORKOUT 86

Walls

My tip for painting walls is quite simple. Look at the dry-stone wall in **Work-out 87**, and you will see the dark areas in the spaces between the stones. **Work-out 88** is of a brick wall; the gaps between the bricks are light, giving the feeling of mortar.

Viewfinder

A viewfinder will help you locate and position your picture. It will also help you to decide how much landscape you want in the picture. Here, I have devised two L-shaped cut-outs (*see* **Work-out 89**) which can be used as adjustable viewfinders. Lay the Ls flat on to the picture as illustrated, and move them from left to right, finding the weakest area in your picture and then cutting it out by making the aperture larger or smaller. Whatever size you end up with is the framing size of your painting. I find that the Ls give a painting suffering from weak composition a second chance.

Boats

It has always been difficult for novices to paint dinghies successfully. I have devised an aid which uses the concept of the early Christian 'fish symbol'. In **Work-out 90**, the fish is swimming towards the centre of the page, and in **Work-out 91** it also swims towards the centre but in the opposite direction.

The drawings here are self-explanatory. Depending on your perspective, your fish will either be fatter or thinner than those shown. Using the symbol you will now be able to create a dinghy which will float, not sink!

Painting from Photographs

When painting from photographs you are in danger of committing the composition error, which many photographers make, of capturing half a tree, as shown in **Work-out 92**. The feeling you get when looking at this picture is that it has been chopped off. By bringing the tree into the picture, a better composition develops, as in **Work-out 93**. Do not be afraid to play God for a day and make the odd change to the landscape to improve your picture.

Work-out 94 is a reminder that just as you have foreground, middle distance and far distance in your landscape, so you must have it in your sky, number 1 being foreground and number 3 distance. A tip here is to remember that within your foreground, middle distance and far distance, you have many more foregrounds, middle distances and far distances. For example, the tree in **Work-out 94** has been extracted

121

WORKOUT 87

WORKOUT 88

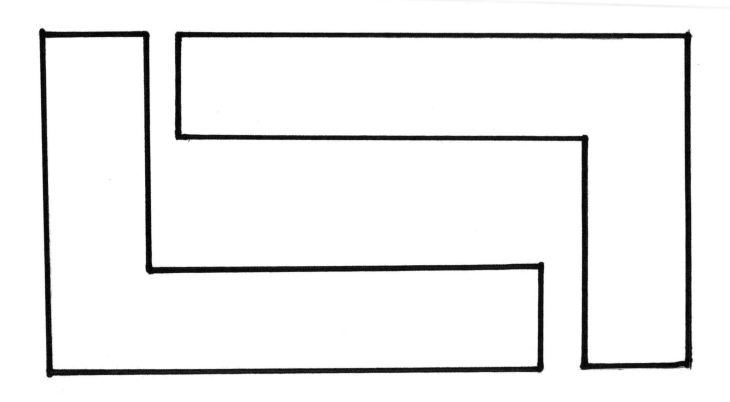

WORKOUT 89

WORKOUT 90

WORKOUT 91

WORKOUT 92

WORKOUT 93

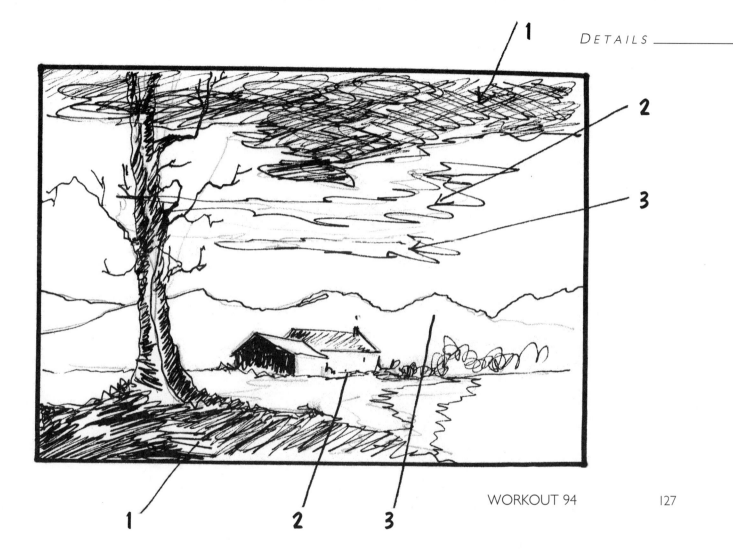

1

2

3

1

2

3

and illustrated in **Work-out 95**, which shows clearly the foreground, middle distance and distance comprising twigs and grass.

Never forget that the trinity of foreground, middle distance and distance repeats itself many, many times in a picture. Remember this and your painting will always have depth.

Cartwheels

When you look at paintings in an exhibition, be it professional or amateur, you will see that many artists fall into the trap of painting what I call 'cartwheels'. Cartwheels weaken a painting and they occur when all points end on the same plane, be it foreground, middle distance or far distance. Consider **Work-out 96**, a painting of a cottage, a track and a wall with hills in the distance. The hill upon which the cottage stands ends at the same point as the road ends; if you look further, you will see that even the walls end at this point too. The spokes of a wheel are formed – the cartwheel. The overall effect this gives is of an absence of space between each plane, and the painting appears flat. You can improve matters and enhance depth by the use of colour, but you will never be able to remove the tell-tale signs completely.

In **Work-out 97**, I have drawn arrows to indicate that not everything should end at the same point. There is no cartwheel here. All lines intersect one another and do not terminate on the same strand or plane.

Bridges

A final tip concerns painting bridges. Do not approach the subject face on, as in **Work-out 98**, as it will make your painting of the bridge flat and the overall appearance look like a cut-out. In the same way you will find that a portrait of a person painted face on can look like a mask.

In **Work-out 99** you will see that I have painted the bridge at an angle and made it more interesting. This allows the viewer to walk over the bridge instead of approaching it from the wrong angle.

Most of the tips in this book are not taught at art school. At art school you learn the strokes and how to swim from the side of the pool. But one of the best and most important arts to master is that of floating – and this you can only achieve with constant practice and experience. It is only by walking in the countryside and observing everything around me that I have been able to formulate these work-out exercises.

Rain on Flushhouse Moor
The finely detailed telegraph poles in this painting lead the eye into the picture, providing perspective and depth.
Incidentally, the poles do exist on the moor in real life!

WORKOUT 95

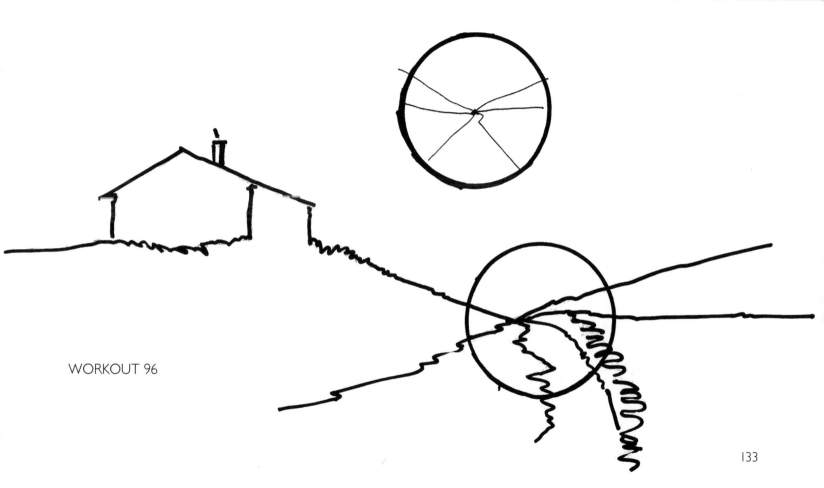

WORKOUT 96

133

WORKOUT 97

WORKOUT 98

WORKOUT 99

Bills' O' Jacks, Dovestones

A FINAL WORD

I have always been told that luck is a measure of the material things in life. For me, however, the greatest luck I have had in life is good health. As a fine artist you have to be self-employed, and being self-employed one cannot afford to be unhealthy.

In other areas of my life I have been blessed with good fortune. One example of this was in 1969 when I was in my gallery in Barnsley and the late artist L.S. Lowry walked in unannounced. I said to Mr Lowry, it was as if Jesus Christ had walked through my door.

He modestly replied, 'I'm only human, lad!'

The good fortune was that he purchased one of my paintings, which was entitled, fittingly, 'Where Counties Meet'. The painting was a moorland scene showing a series of wooden poles, parish boundary markings, traversing the moor. From that day on, he and I were friends, and he was, and always will be, my mentor.

Lowry gave me much sound advice. On one occasion I talked to him on the subject of gaining letters after one's name. He said, 'Never ever ask to join a society, sir, because it gives them the right to refuse you; if you wait until they ask you, you have the right to refuse them!'

In the mid-1970s, when I have having a one-man exhibition in the West End of London, I was invited to 10 Downing Street to meet the Prime Minister of the day, Harold Wilson. There on the lounge wall hung one of old man Lowry's paintings. The Prime Minister commented, 'You know this gentleman very well, don't you?' I replied, 'Yes'. The Prime Minister continued: 'I offered him a Knighthood, he turned it down, I offered him the Companion of Honour, and he turned that down too.' Apart from his mother whom he loved dearly, all Lowry cared about was his art. What did such labels matter?

On another occasion Lowry said to me: 'Never ever paint for critics. Always paint to please yourself, because if they could paint, Ashley, they wouldn't be critics.'

His words have carried me through my life as an artist, and now I can pass them on to you.

My greatest pleasure and excitement is to be able to put down in colour what the eye, the mind and the body can see and feel. A painting is then universal, and can be 'read' not only by academics but by the illiterate – any human being, irrespective of creed or colour. The beauty about painting is that it erects no barriers, either religious or political. It is one of the most beautiful gifts which marks out the human being from the animal. That is why I do what I do, painting what I want, how I feel, and how others feel, capturing the atmosphere of our beautiful world.

I leave you with this anecdote about the effect on my painting by a person who had no artistic temperament and could not paint. I met a shepherd once while out painting a mountainside in England, and we struck up a conversation. Speaking about the incredible skyscapes that exist, he said, 'Many people try and capture these large and powerful rain clouds, and because they haven't studied them properly, they look like cows' udders in the sky.' I have tried ever since not to put udders in my skies!

INDEX

Page numbers in *italics* refer to illustrations

ACKNOWLEDGEMENTS

I would like to thank Heather, my daughter, for her vision
and patience while typing and editing this book.
I would also like to thank Susanna Wadeson of Boxtree
for giving me the help and support I have needed to
produce this book.

PUBLISHERS' NOTE

The Publishers wish to apologise for the following errors in this edition of
A BRUSH WITH ASHLEY:

Page 52: A double L composition may he found in Work-out 14, not Work-out
18 as is stated.

Pages 52, 58, 62: the illustrations for Work-outs 31 and 33, and for 32 and 34
have been transposed. For Work-out 31 see the illustration marked Work-out
33 and vice versa; for Work-out 32 see Work-out 34 and vice versa.

Pages 66 and 82: Please note the illustrations on these pages have been transposed. For Work-out 38b see the illustration on page 82; for Work-out 53 see
the illustration on page 66.

Page 93: The Work-out which appears on page 93 is Work-out 60.